Bygone
UCKFIELD

'Old Bridge at Uckfield', built in 1617 and taken down in 1859.

Bygone
UCKFIELD

Barbara Fuller
and Betty Turner

Phillimore

1988

Published by
PHILLIMORE & CO. LTD.
Shopwyke Hall, Chichester, Sussex

© Barbara Fuller and Betty Turner, 1988

ISBN 0 85033 680 5

Printed and bound in Great Britain by
BIDDLES LTD.
Guildford, Surrey

*To the memory of Frank Fuller
and Frederick and Annie Bellingham*

List of Illustrations

Frontispiece: Print of the 'Old Bridge at Uckfield'

Acknowledgments

The authors are grateful to the following who loaned photographs for reproduction in this book: Mr. G. W. Ashman, nos. 113 and 133; Miss Shelagh Dalton, no. 72; Mr. Norman Edwards, nos. 71, 84 a and b, and 120; Mr. L. Frisby, nos. 1, 2, 156, and 157; Mr. S. N. Hughes, nos. 107, and 126; Mr. E. Jack Johnson, nos. 76 and 77; Miss K. Pierpoint, nos. 53 and 108; Mrs. Edie Siggs, no. 54; Miss Ruth Spencer, no. 148; Mr. Gerald Standen, no. 150; Mrs. Joan Williams, nos. 163 and 164. Numbers 78, 97 and 127 are reproduced from Pike's *Views and Reviews* and the endpaper advertisements are from *Brooker's 1888 Guide and Directory for Uckfield and District.*

Introduction

Many people might not realise the extent of Uckfield's history, owing partly perhaps to the fact that it was not mentioned in Domesday Book. But several of this typical small Sussex town's neighbouring villages were listed in the 1086 survey, including Flescinges (Fletching), Mesefeld (Maresfield), Framelle (Framfield) and Horstede (Little Horsted), the last two being in the Manor of Framelle held by Robert, Earl of Mortain, in the rape of Pevensey, and certainly within a little over a hundred years it had become a place of some importance.

The derivation of the town's name is a matter for speculation as it appears in at least two different forms, as Okenfield and Okyngfeld. This gives rise to the suggestion that it was known as the place with the 'oak in the field', and, although this area lies within a sand formation, there are sufficient patches of clay, favoured by oaks, in the district to make this a feasible theory. Another theory, equally feasible, is that it derives from the Celtic 'Uch', meaning 'Upper' as opposed to 'Is' meaning 'Lower'. Isfield, a neighbouring village lower down the river, gives credibility to this theory.

In the 13th century, Uckfield is referred to as a vill or part of the parish of Buxted. Indeed, the parish church of Uckfield was a chapel-of-ease to Buxted church until 1846. Even so, Uckfield did gain some importance due to its location on the road from Canterbury to Chichester; it became a resting-place for pilgrims making this journey. There was, supposedly, a Bishop's Palace situated on what is now Luxfords Field in the centre of the town, and Church Street, being part of this route, was the first area of concentrated habitation in Uckfield. Edward I, too, apparently stayed overnight in Uckfield in the year 1299, staying with one 'Arnald de Uckfield'. According to the records of his steward, he purchased large quantities of ale and poultry.

A crypt or dungeon was once situated beneath a building on the southern corner of Church Street. Legend says that the Sussex Protestant martyr, Richard Woodman, was imprisoned there on his way to Lewes to be burnt at the stake in the reign of Queen Mary. Certainly, the iron rings in the wall suggested the building may have been used as a prison, but the arches and recesses pointed to an original ecclesiastical use. Sadly, this ancient building, like so many others in Uckfield, has been demolished. Bridge Cottage alone, of all Uckfield's historic sites, has survived, thanks to the intervention of the preservation society.

Although Uckfield is not thought to have been immediately involved in the iron industry, neighbouring parishes certainly were. The first iron cannon was cast by Ralph Hogge at Buxted in 1543, and Maresfield parish had at least three forges at Powder Mills, Old Forge and Oldlands, Fairwarp. In 1793, when the Upper Ouse Navigation Canal was completed, barges could come up as far as Shortbridge and were used for the transportation of iron products, thus saving the iron-masters the heavy tolls on the turnpike roads. The development of the railways ended the viability of the canal, which closed in 1868.

The railway, however, encouraged the growth of Uckfield. The line from Brighton and Lewes to Uckfield was opened in 1858, and in 1866 it was completed to Groombridge and Tunbridge Wells, giving Uckfield a link with London. It brought the town out of rural isolation and took goods and passengers daily to places previously out of reach. The first railway excursion left Uckfield at 8.30 a.m. on 24 July 1859 to Portsmouth, the fares being 10s. first class, 5s. 6d. second, and 3s. in a covered wagon. It was planned to open two further lines – one to Haywards Heath, via Newick, and the other to East Hoathly, Hailsham and Eastbourne. Neither line materialised, although a start was actually made on the one to Haywards Heath.

In any event, the coming of the railway brought expansion to the business and farming communities in the area. Corn, hops, chickens and roses were sent by rail, several new shops were opened, including a new fishmonger's which was able to offer 'fresh fish from Billingsgate daily', not possible before the railway. Coal was brought to the town by train and, in 1859, the gasworks were built, bringing gas-lighting to the streets of Uckfield. The brickworks turned over to coal and faggots were phased out. In 1882, W. H. Smith's bookstall opened on the station.

The railway also brought about an expansion in building. Several good sites were made available both to the north and south of the town, and many larger, fashionable villas were built south of the railway for use as private accommodation or apartments. This area became known as High Street, New Town. Several of these houses took their names from Lake District towns – Westmorland House, Ennerdale Lodge, Ulverston House. Thomas Bannister, grocer, draper, outfitter, furniture warehouseman and undertaker, also opened new premises at Albion House, New Town, obviously intending to supply every need of Uckfield's new middle-class populace. The eighth public house, the *Railway Tavern*, also opened south of the line in 1888, on the opposite corner to the new Congregational church, built in 1866. Uckfield catered for both the sinner and the saint.

Smaller houses were built in Framfield Road and Mr. Henry Hudson, a local builder of No. 20, Alexandra Road , was responsible for building freehold terrace houses, Nos. 21-32 Alexandra Road, which sold at auction at the *Star Inn*, Lewes, at approximately £125 each. Both brickmakers in the town (Messrs. Ware & Sons and Tyhurst & Son) prospered from the increase in trade and the expansion in building.

Thus, the railway brought an air of prosperity and growth to Uckfield in the second half of the 19th century. The 1869 *Visitors' Guide* described Uckfield as a healthy place where the air was exceptionally clear. This was borne out by the fact that there were two observatories in the town, one belonging to Charles Leeson Prince, a doctor, who wrote a book entitled *The Climate of Uckfield from 1843-1870*, and the other to Mr. F. Brodie, a local magistrate. With the advent of the motor car, Uckfield's central position between Tunbridge Wells, Brighton and Eastbourne brought many visitors to enjoy the surrounding picturesque scenery and to attend the steeplechases which were held at Blackdown on the Streatfeild Rocks Estate.

The London, Brighton & South Coast Railway, as it was first called, continued until 1923 when it was absorbed by the Southern Railway, and on 1 January 1948 it became part of British Railways on nationalisation. Following the rapid increase in car ownership and the need for a by-pass for Lewes for which railway land was required, the last through train from Tunbridge Wells to Brighton ran in October 1968. To this day, there has never ceased to be a nucleus of residents in Uckfield who dream of seeing that Uckfield to Lewes line opened again. Instead, on 6 July 1985 the last train ran from Uckfield to Tunbridge Wells West, leaving Uckfield to Oxted the only remaining line.

There were, of course, changes brought about by the two World Wars, during which Uckfield and district played host to the Army at Maresfield Camp in the Park from 1914 to 1918, and in Batts Road from 1941 to 1945. In 1937, two large council housing estates were built at Selby Rise and Church Coombe by Uckfield R.D.C. In 1964, Uckfield changed beyond recognition when planning permission was quite unexpectedly granted for Manor Park Estate and in a few short years the population doubled. Since then, further estates have sprung up and more are planned.

Most travellers by road since the end of the Second World War remember the frustration of sitting in traffic queues in the High Street when the railway level-crossing gates closed, and every summer, holiday and day-tripper traffic jams led to 30 minute journeys to get from Ringles Cross or Union Point into the town. However, in 1985, after 50 years on and off the drawing board, the Uckfield by-pass arrived to alleviate these problems and to give Uckfield a re-birth.

Uckfield is still trying to cater for its ever-expanding population. The 1869 *Visitors' Guide* ends its chapter on Uckfield with these words: 'But there is yet one necessity affecting the future of Uckfield – and the blessings of the rising generation will attend whoever assists to remove it – we mean the establishment of a public swimming bath'. One hundred and eighteen years later Uckfield got its swimming pool, plus a Leisure Centre. There is still an Uckfield Cinema, built in 1916, the longest continuously-running cinema in the county. The town has retained its wonderful hospital, and there are hopes for its future expansion, as well as plans for a new town centre development and supermarket, and for a new community centre and town hall.

There is much to look forward to but, meanwhile, we present this nostalgic collection of photographs which we hope will give pleasure to all – happy memories for the older townsfolk and a glimpse of what Uckfield was once like for the new residents.

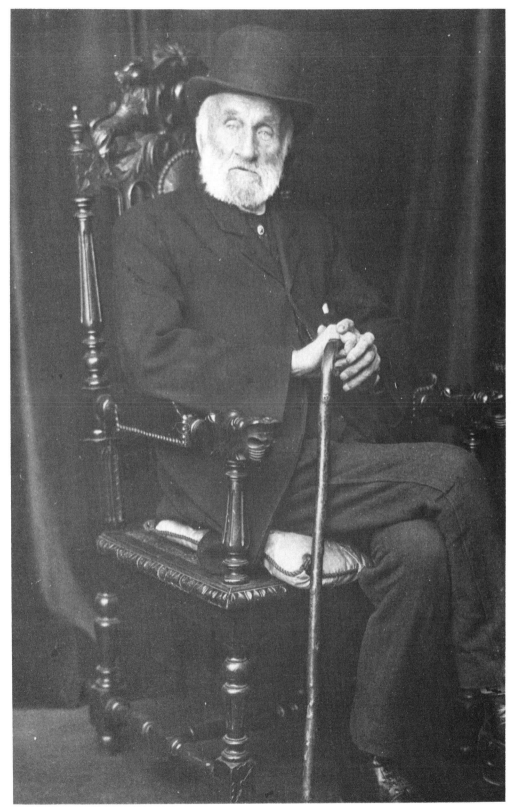

1. Mr. John Frisby, one of the most important early photographers of Uckfield. He lived at No. 6 Birdnye Terrace, Framfield Road, and recorded for posterity many scenes, personalities and events in the town. The following photographs are known to be by Mr. Frisby: Nos. 10, 22, 25, 28, 37, 53, 94, 97, 111, 127.

2.   Mr. Frisby, carrying his all-important tripod and possibly going to fetch his white pony and trap, which he kept at the Alma, Framfield Road. The child who can just be seen walking behind him is carrying the photographic plates. Mr. Frisby died in 1929, leaving a wonderful pictorial history of Uckfield before the First World War.

Townscapes

3. General view of Uckfield from the south, 1871. The buildings which can be seen, mostly still in existence, formed the nucleus of the New Town, which developed considerably after the completion of the railway in 1866.

4. South corner of Church Street, c.1890. The old house and shop on the lower corner were pulled down in 1891, and under this property was a crypt, or dungeon, known locally as the 'Bishop's prison'. Legend says that Richard Woodman, a famous Sussex martyr burnt at Lewes in the reign of Queen Mary, was imprisoned here.

5. The same corner of Church Street, *c*.1904, showing the property which replaced the one in the previous photograph. Whiteside's had obviously become a thriving business very quickly.

6. The north corner of Church Street, c.1903. This timber-framed building is faced with mathematical tiles, which give the appearance of brick construction. Note the board over the corner window advertising the stabling at the back of the *Maiden's Head Hotel*.

7. Church Street, looking eastwards, c.1904. The house on the left with the tiled porch was the Catholic priest's house, and the row of cottages on the right was known as 'The Strand'.

8. Copthall. This photograph is a very early one; judging by the crinoline dresses and the gentleman's stove pipe hat, probably about 1860. Gas was introduced to Uckfield in 1859 so the new lamp post may have prompted the photograph.

9. A later photograph of Copthall. A third house has been added to the previous two.

10.   The cottages known as 'White Rails'. These cottages, built of local stone, were situated on the left hand side of the High Street, looking north. The cottages were pulled down in 1898 and another row of brick-built terrace houses replaced them. These in turn were demolished in 1960 except for the last two, which now house a Building Society and a greengrocery.

11.   High Street, *c.*1910. The post office, on the right, was built in 1896 and remained there until a new post office was built in its present position in 1930. The first manual telephone exchange was opened in the building shown here in 1905 with just two operators. The site is now occupied by Carvills Furnishings.

Uckfield, High Street.

12.   High Street, looking south, and showing the shop owned by Mr. Harcourt Smith, the local bookbinder and publisher who also ran the shop as a Library. In the early 1950s the Secondary Modern School was opened and the County Council Library was held there until a purpose-built structure was opened in the centre of the town in the 1960s.

13.   The upper part of the High Street, *c.*1900. Of particular interest is the muffin man with his tray balanced on his head. He would ring his bell as he went along to announce his presence and to attract trade. Note also the very high kerbs with the small steps at regular intervals.

High Street Uckfield. 1900

CHESTNUT TREE,
HIGH STREET, UCKFIELD.

14. Further up the High Street, showing the beautiful chestnut tree in full bloom. Sadly, this tree, such a landmark in the Uckfield townscape, was destroyed by the hurricane-force storm on 16 October 1987.

15. London Road, c.1905, in the days of flintstone road surfacing. On the right can be seen heaps of flints ready for use. The houses on the left were new at this time as they were built between 1900 and 1904 and were described as high-class residences.

16. Mr. Hollyman's Furniture Store, situated where the Southdown Hatcheries were for many years.

17. Mr. Hollyman's Furniture and Draper's shop on the opposite side of the road, c.1910. Mr. Hollyman became engaged to be married, but just before the wedding it was discovered that his fiancée was his sister. The wedding was called off and the bride-to-be eventually became his housekeeper.

18. *Ringles Cross Hotel, c.*1905, advertising 'good accommodation for cyclists' in the days when traffic consisted mainly of the horse and cart.

19. A much busier scene at Ringles Cross in about 1925, showing a well-attended car rally.

20.   Union Point, at the southern end of Uckfield, with the populace turning out to cheer the gallant walkers.

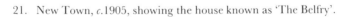

21.   New Town, *c*.1905, showing the house known as 'The Belfry'.

22. The Agricultural College. A High School was established here in 1881 which was purchased by the East Sussex County Council in 1894 and turned into an Agricultural College, the first of its kind in the area. The buildings were commandeered by the Army during both world wars, and betweeen the wars it was run as a preparatory school called St Michael's College.

23. Troops outside the commandeered Agricultural College in 1915. Daily life continued unchanged, though, as shown by Mr. Ashdown delivering milk in his handcart.

24. New Town, showing the *Railway Tavern*, which opened in 1888 on the corner of Framfield Road. This brought the number of public houses in the town to eight. The blind next door shades a little sweet shop from the sun.

25. New Town, looking north, *c.*1900. The large doors on the left belonged to the Volunteer Fire Brigade Station, and just beyond the signal box can be seen Mr. Brooker's wheelwright's workshop which became the site of Uckfield bus station. (*See* photo No. 59.)

26.   A photograph showing the start of the earthworks for the construction of Mill Drove in the early 1900s. The cottage and shop at the bottom of the hill, belonging to Bourners the local carriers and coal merchants, is now the site of Caffyns Garage.

27.   The Uckfield Town Band on parade, passing the now well-established Mill Drove, plus houses and shops which are very little changed today.

28.   Bridge Cottage, *c.*1912. This is probably the oldest surviving house in Uckfield, built between 1380 and 1420. For nearly four centuries it was quite a substantial farmhouse, called Bridge Farm, but in the 19th century it was made into two dwellings for workers and their families. It remained a dwelling place until 1966, but is now the main centre of the Uckfield Preservation Society, which has restored it to its original attractive appearance.

29.   High Street, *c.*1904. On the right can be seen the entrance gate to the Uckfield Stock Market which opened in 1895 and was held every alternate Wednesday for the sale of cattle, poultry, eggs and farm produce. Twice a year a Fat Stock Show was held. It finally closed in 1931. Next to the entrance is the *Bell Hotel*, which was demolished as recently as October 1980 to make way for a supermarket.

30. High Street, *c*.1905. On the extreme right is Mr. T. Brooke's shop – he built the organs for both the parish church and the United Reformed church, then known as the Congregational church.

31. High Street, *c*.1909, showing how, apart from the lack of traffic, the left hand side of the High Street has changed very little over the last 80 years.

32. Pudding Cake Lane. The origin of this name is unknown. This photograph shows it when it really was a lane, a delightful rural walk in the centre of Uckfield, and a well-frequented courting spot on summer Sunday evenings. It was incorporated into Church Coombe housing estate when it was built in 1950.

33. Rocks Road, *c*.1904, at the junction with Snatts Road. This road ran through the middle of the Rocks Estate, which was owned by the Streatfeild family until the death of Annette Streatfeild in 1938. The Estate was then sold, consisting of about 2,115 acres divided into 118 lots. It included many farms, premises in the High Street, 90 cottages, and also the Uckfield Cottage Hospital.

34. Rocks Bridge. This wooden bridge joined the Rocks Estate land on either side of the road, connecting the House to the Estate farm and sawmills.

35. The Rocks House. After Richard Thomas Streatfeild inherited the Copwood Estate in 1770, he pulled down Copwood House and built the first Rocks House. His son, Richard Shuttleworth Streatfeild, demolished the house that his father had built and erected the second Rocks House in 1838. This remained the Streatfeild family home until the death of his grand-daughter, Annette, in 1938.

36.   The funeral procession of the last squire of Uckfield, Richard James Streatfeild, who died on 30 July 1931. His coffin is being carried on one of the estate wagons along Rocks Road on the way to the church.

37.   Birdnye Terrace, Framfield Road, *c.*1905. This row of cottages, fairly new at that time, cost just £60 to buy. They are virtually unchanged today, apart from the addition of a few front porches, but have increased vastly in price.

38.   Framfield Road, *c.*1906. Next to the *Alma Arms* can be seen the Lion Brewery, owned by G. S. Bourner & Co., who were also the local carriers.

39.   The Uckfield Urban District Council road-tarring gang, resting from their labours at the bottom of Harcourt Road. The bowler-hatted gentleman (probably the foreman) sitting on the tar barrel went by the unusual nickname of 'Numbers' Olive, and the man on the extreme right was known as 'Sugar' French.

40. Harcourt Road, *c.*1905. A Friendly Society known as 'The Foresters' had these halls built in 1904. The larger building became the Uckfield Cinema where the youth of Uckfield enjoyed Saturday matinées for 1d. each. In the 1920s it became a dance hall until it was acquired by the East Sussex County Council in about 1935 and used as a cookery and woodworking centre until 1950.

41. A photograph of newly-built Vernon Road, taken by Mr. A. Windsor-Spice, another well-known local artist and photographer. It shows the postman, Mr. Hazelden, outside his house. Mr. Leslie Hazelden, his son, lived there until 1988.

42. The row of substantial, well-built houses known as 'The Croft' in Framfield Road. In 1871, one of the houses was occupied by George Humphrey, the stationmaster, until the station house was ready, so that he was 'accommodated in a dwelling most suited to his social class'.

Hopfields and Breweries

43.   This hopfield was situated to the west of London Road. 'The Cedars' can be seen in the background of this picture. In 1831 Uckfield had three breweries and hop cultivation was fairly extensive. A decline set in around 1850 and only two of the breweries survived – the Uckfield Brewery, situated in Norfolk Place, and the Lion Brewery in Framfield Road (*see* picture no. 38). The latter eventually closed towards the end of the century, but the Uckfield Brewery continued until after the First World War.

44. A winter scene in a hopfield on the outskirts of Uckfield, showing the hop poles waiting to be put up.

45. The prepared hops at Hempstead Farm ready for transport to the Brewery. Mr. Gaius Farrant, sitting on the hop sacks, was employed at the farm for many years.

46.   More activity at Hempstead Farm Oast.

47.   The Uckfield hopgardens, showing the variety of splendid hats worn by the ladies working in the fields. The small boy in the smock, standing by the hop bin, is the late Mr. James Scott, co-founder of the firm of Fuller & Scott.

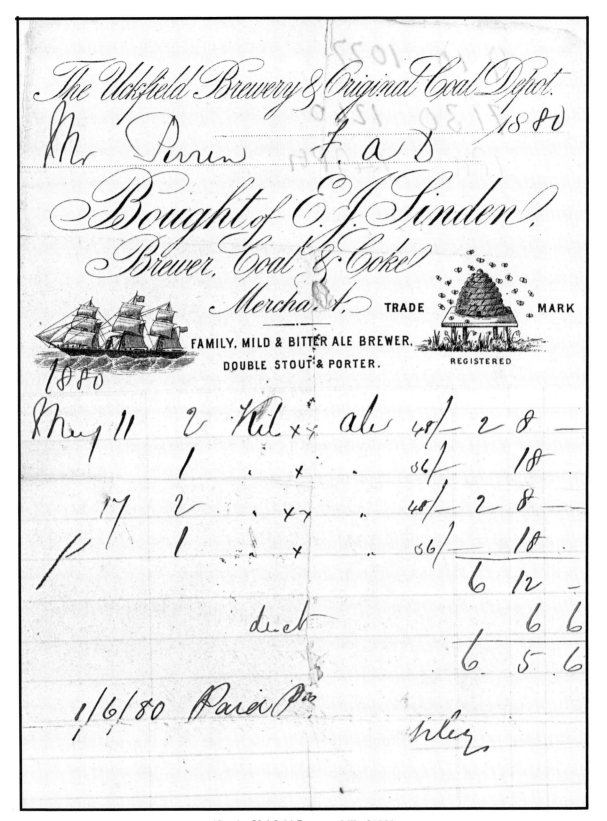

The Uckfield Brewery & Original Coal Depot.

1880

Mr Perren F a d

Bought of E. J. Sinden,

Brewer, Coal & Coke

Merchant, TRADE MARK

FAMILY, MILD & BITTER ALE BREWER,
DOUBLE STOUT & PORTER.

REGISTERED

1880

May 11	2	Kil ×× ale	40/	2	8	—
	1	" × "	36/		18	
17	2	" ×× "	40/	2	8	—
	1	" × "	36/		18	
				6	12	—
		dedt			6	6
				6	5	6

1/6/80 Paid P.

48.   An Uckfield Brewery bill of 1880.

49. Another view of the Uckfield hopgardens.

Transport

50. The horse bus, *c.*1902. Mr. Charles Catt of Nutley started the first local public transport system in 1902 – a horse bus which ran from the *Nutley Inn* to Uckfield Railway Station and back. It made a once-daily run throughout the year (twice on Saturdays), leaving Nutley at 8.45 a.m. and taking about an hour to reach Uckfield on the bad roads. The fare was 1s. 6d. return or 10d. single.

51. Uckfield railway station, *c.*1915. Note the mounted soldier on the right, probably from Maresfield Camp, and the cabby with his taxi cab, waiting for customers from the next train.

52. Another photograph of the railway station, with something approaching a horse-drawn traffic jam!

53. Bourner & Co., seen here opposite the railway station, were Railway & General Carriers, and Merchants for corn, seeds, hay, straw, oil-cake and cotton-cake. They were also furniture removers and could supply pair-horse brakes for pleasure, cricket and other parties within a 20-mile radius of Uckfield. Caffyns Garage now occupies the site of their premises.

54. The gas bag. Another form of transport outside the *Bridge Hotel* (now the *Prince Regent*). The gas bag was used during the First World War when petrol was unavailable, and the vehicle was driven to the Gas Works to be refilled. Note the two original Brighton registration numbers on the vehicles, and also the plate glass window of the Coffee Room which is still in position today.

55.   The collapse of the bridge next to the railway station on 27 June 1903, when a traction engine owned by the East Sussex County Council fell through into the river. The driver, a Mr. Wright, fortunately received only a cracked rib and minor bruises.

56. Repairs to the bridge being carried out, watched by a gathering of local dignitaries.

57. A much later photograph but one of historic interest. This was the last steam train to leave Uckfield before the 'soulless' diesels took over.

58. Dr. Sweet's car, a 1905 Humber driven by Mr. Dutson, chauffeur.

59. The workshops of James S. Brooker, wheelwright and carpenter, c.1890. These stood on what was to become for many years the site of the Southdown Bus Station, before it too was demolished in order to bring the line of shops right up to the edge of the link-road to the by-pass.

60. The Uckfield bus terminus, c.1922, showing three beautiful examples of the buses of the day, still running on solid tyres, and the front one clearly destined for Lewes and Brighton. The drinking fountain on the left was erected to the memory of the late Rector, Rev. E. T. Cardale, in 1894. When the Drill Hall, built behind it in 1908, was demolished to make way for retail development, the fountain was removed to the Victoria recreation ground.

61. Two aeroplanes came down in a field near the Uckfield recreation ground on 2 July 1911. This, the second, crash-landed, causing minor damage, whilst coming down to investigate the first plane, flown by Mr. Gordon England, who had merely landed to check his petrol as there were no petrol gauges in those days. Eventually, with help from Mr. England, the plane left Uckfield the next day.

62.   This photograph shows, on the right, Mr. Eddie Ellsley, driver of the first Southdown bus between Uckfield and Brighton. One of his relations was a co-founder of the Southdown Bus Company in Brighton and Mr. Ellsley started his driving career there. But when the service was extended to Uckfield, he and his wife moved into lodgings in the town and he became a regular driver on the Uckfield to Brighton route. The man on the left is Mr. Wood, nicknamed 'Splinters', who was the conductor and relief driver when needed.

Retail Trade

63. Fuller's was a well-established bakery situated in Church Street. During the 1914-18 War, the daughters of the family all helped by delivering bread in these delightful handcarts. This photograph is of Phyllis Fuller. Mrs. Fuller, besides looking after a family of eight, ran the shop and tea rooms, which were well patronised by the Canadian troops, situated in Maresfield Camp.

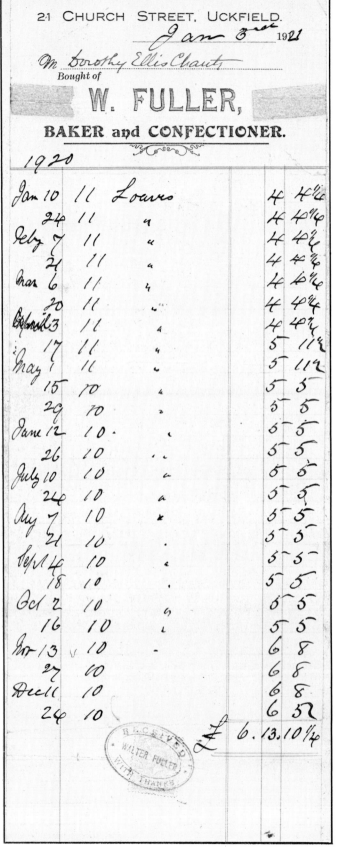

21 CHURCH STREET, UCKFIELD.

Jan 3rd 1921

Mr Dorothy Ellis Charity
Bought of

W. FULLER,
BAKER and CONFECTIONER.

1920

Jan 10	11	Loaves	4	4½¼
24	11	"	4	4½¼
Feby 7	11	"	4	4½¼
21	11	"	4	4½¼
Mar 6	11	"	4	4½¼
20	11	"	4	4½¼
April 3	11	"	4	4½¼
17	11	"	5	11½
May 1	11	"	5	11½
15	10	"	5	5
29	10	"	5	5
June 12	10	"	5	5
26	10	"	5	5
July 10	10	"	5	5
24	10	"	5	5
Aug 7	10	"	5	5
21	10	"	5	5
Sept 4	10	"	5	5
18	10	"	5	5
Oct 2	10	"	5	5
16	10	"	5	5
Nov 13	10	"	6	8
27	10		6	8
Dec 11	10		6	8
24	10		6	5½

£ 6. 13. 10¼

64. A 1921 bread bill. The same amount of bread today would cost more than £130! The bill is in the name of the Dorothy Ellis Charity. Miss Ellis was a philanthropic spinster of Lewes who died in 1731, leaving £300 to be invested by three trustees. Some of the profits were to be spent on 12 fourpenny loaves to be given to 12 poor families every other Sunday at Uckfield parish church.

65. Mr. William Dendy's shop, *c.*1902, today trading as Cullens. This building was up for sale in 1792 at the *White Hart Hotel* in Lewes as a farmhouse, with 82 acres of land, and including a cottage in Hempstead Lane. The reserve price for this lot was £500. It was bought by the Manchester Cotton Co. for the sum of £630, hence the name 'Manchester House'.

66. 'Manchester House', c.1922. The grocery side of Mr. Dendy's business was managed by Mr. Wilde, who, on Mr. Dendy's death, purchased first the grocery shop and later the whole premises. The business was continued by Mr. Leslie Wilde until it was taken over by Cullens.

67. A fine showing of Southdown lamb and fat stock produce outside Thurston's butcher's shop, around 1912. Mr. Thurston can be seen at the door, knife in hand. This shop is still a butcher's today, still trading as Thurstons, under the ownership of the Swain family.

68. One of Mr. Cartwright's splendid Christmas displays, 1908. He was the local fishmonger and remained as such until well after the Second World War.

69. Another well-established Uckfield family – the Barfords. Mr. Barford purchased these premises in 1899 for £300, and this photograph shows Mrs. Barford on the left in the doorway, with son Val and daughter Jessie standing outside. This shop was next to the *Kings Head*, which is now the Cinque Ports Club.

70. Thomas H. Barford later moved his business to bigger and better premises further down the High Street, and added a Gentleman's Outfitters just below the opposite corner of Grange Road. This family business flourished until 1980.

71. Bannister's Stores, *c.*1905. This shows the furniture department which was situated opposite Albion House and its adjacent warehouse in New Town, where Thomas Bannister Snr. started his business as grocer, draper, outfitter, furniture warehouseman and undertaker in the mid-19th century. He was joined in the business by his son, Thomas Bannister Jnr., who later closed all but the furniture department, which eventually passed into the hands of Miss Phyllis Bannister. It was badly damaged by fire in the 1950s and, not long after its re-building, Miss Bannister sold the business.

72. Sidney Oddie started his pharmacy business at 80/82 High Street, New Town, early in the century and after the Second World War transferred to a more central position at 162 High Street where the business continued into the 1970s. Mr. Oddie took a partner and traded as Oddie & Whitby for some years. Mrs. M. E. Oddie was an artist and one of her paintings hangs on the stairway in the Uckfield Hospital.

SYDNEY ODDIE, M.P.S.

Dispensing and Photographic Chemist and Optician

Depôt for
REXALL
   Remedies.
Toilet
   Requisites.
All KODAK
   supplies.
ARTISTS'
   Materials.

Depôt for

Veterinary,

Agricultural
and
Horticultural

Preparations.

NEW TOWN PHARMACY (opposite Railway Station),
80 and 82 HIGH STREET, UCKFIELD.

DEVELOPING AND PRINTING FOR AMATEURS.   EYESIGHT TESTED.
ARTISTIC ARTICLES FOR GIFTS.   TELEPHONE 50.

73. The coming of the Co-operative Society to Uckfield, in Framfield Road,
on 21 March 1906. Such an important event obviously caused the ladies to bring
out their best hats – a truly wonderful array.

74. Bellingham's Temperance Hotel, 106 High Street, later known as 'The Central Tea Rooms', which provided the outside catering for most of the town's functions in the early years of the century. Later the premises became a wool and children's clothes shop, the last of the proprietors being Margaret Phillips, daughter of Mr. Cornwall who was Seedman at 109 High Street for many years.

The Brickworks

75. Pottery Cottages, New Road, Ridgewood. These were cottages built for the employees of the potteries, the firm adopting a practice pioneered by Robert Owen, cotton manufacturer and social reformer in the early 19th century, and furthered by such national figures as the Cadburys and the Lever Brothers. The firm eventually closed down in the early 1970s, the buildings were demolished and a small industrial estate now covers the site.

76. Messrs. Ware's delivery wagon. The steam engine towed a trailer to deliver bricks and tiles from the brickyard to the customers. Bert Walls, the driver, is showing his engine to young Master Ernest Lillywhite, with Harry Lillywhite looking on.

77. The workforce of the Sussex Pottery Brick & Tile Works, Ridgewood. The firm was first established in 1770, and for about the last 130 years of its life was run by the Ware family, initially Benjamin Ware. They did considerable business in Sussex and Hampshire in horticultural pottery, bricks, pipes and tiles, their output of flowerpots alone being between 30,000 and 40,000 per week. The works covered an area of eight acres and employed over 50 workmen.

Other Uckfield Businesses

78.   Uckfield Roller Mills. In the reign of Elizabeth I, John Warnett held the Uckfield Mill, and this was recorded on a 1724 map of Sussex. In 1849 it was bought by Mr. William Kenward, and his son, Edward, began the process of modernisation when he took over in 1874. He built the larger of the three buildings, on the left, to accommodate the new plant, replacing the old water-powered millstone system which was still retained in the old buildings as an auxiliary.

79.   Hempstead Mill, *c.* 1909, referred to as Hemstedmyll as far back as 1543. It was also one of the water mills that made use of the Upper Ouse Navigation until its decline in the mid-19th century. The mill continued working until after the Second World War. The young girl in the picture is Dorrie Homewood, who lived at the mill.

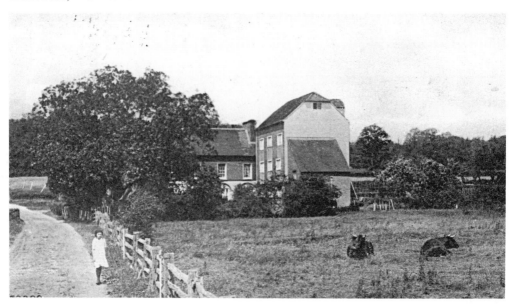

80. A group of Sussex Chicken Fatters near Uckfield.

81. The Uckfield Steam Laundry was situated in Framfield Road, and continued in the ownership of the same family until the early 1960s.

82. Private enterprise at its purest. This sweep, pushing his tricycle up Uckfield High Street, was named William Page and lived in Church Street.

83. A. D. West's Woodyard in Framfield Road. Such woodyards were a common sight in this area, where the art of coppicing was practised, hoops for barrels were made, and pea, bean and flower sticks were supplied. The house on the left looks most strange to modern eyes, as it is now a double dwelling, the second house having been added at a later date.

84a. & b.   Basil Johnson, a well-known Uckfield character, with his banner in the High Street. As well as being in business as an Insurance Agent, Mr. Johnson was a fervent and dedicated evangelist, often to be seen on Brighton sea-front with his message, or touring around the local villages with a small group of followers, holding prayer meetings in the open air. They took with them a miniature portable harmonium to accompany the hymns.

Basil Johnson,

AGENCY for
ALL KINDS OF
INSURANCE

30 HARCOURT ROAD
UCKFIELD.

ENQUIRIES RESPECTFULLY SOLICITED.

Public Amenities

Mr G. EARL *(Asst. Clerk).* Mr G. E. HART *(Asst. Clerk).* Mr W. HOLMES Mr C. THOMPSON *(Surveyor).*

Mr J. WILKINSON Mr W. DENDY Mr E. H. DADSWELL Mr J. JENNER Mr C. DAWSON *(Clerk).* Mr H. RICE Mr E. KENWARD

Mr T. BANNISTER Mr R. L. THORNTON Mr R. J. STREATFEILD *(Chairman).* Mr S. S. AVIS *(Vice-Chairman).* Mr B. WARE

85. The Uckfield Urban District Council, 1896-7. The majority of these stalwart gentlemen are well-remembered names in Uckfield, including Charles Dawson, renowned for the Piltdown Man hoax. The rest were mainly businessmen of the town, with Squire Streatfeild as the Chairman.

86. High View House, previously known as the Union Workhouse. *Whitings Directory* of 1869 claims that it was 'situated on a healthful and commanding position'. This may have been true, as an item in the parish magazine for October 1892 states: 'At the end of October, four old people died in the Workhouse. Their ages were 94, 89, 85 and 80, making an aggregate of 348 years'.

87. The Public Hall, built and furnished in 1877 at a cost of £2,000, with money raised by a public company promoted principally by the magistrates of the Uckfield Bench, who needed better accommodation for the petty sessions than the *Maiden's Head Hotel*. The Hall was also available to the public 'for meetings, balls, concerts and entertainments'. It was extended in 1907 to its present size.

88.　Major extension work at the Uckfield Sewage Works, September 1927. At this time the works were situated just beyond the end of Belmont Lane. When Uckfield expanded, a larger sewage plant was built further south, beyond the old railway line. Standing at the back are: (left to right) Bert Olive, Mr. Brumsden, Mr. Lee, Stationmaster, Mr. Bridger and Mr. Hollis, Surveyor. Standing in the bottom of the tank are Laurie Johnson and Bill North.

89. The cemetery in Snatts Road. The Burial Board for the Parish acquired three acres of land, laid out the grounds and erected two chapels at a cost of £1,100, partly with borrowed money and partly with parish funds. The chapel, devoted to the use of Church of England members, was consecrated by the Bishop of Chichester on 30 August 1884, and the first interment took place on 19 January 1885.

90. The old cottages known as 'The Old Workhouse'. Nothing is known of the early history of this workhouse but the brick and tiled cottage is still inhabited today and is known as Bell Farm. The thatched cottage was pulled down c.1930.

91.   The Uckfield fire brigade, *c.*1905. An entry in an 1869 *Uckfield Guide* said: 'An excellent fire engine has recently been purchased by public subscription and a volunteer fire brigade is being established'. This is that brigade nearly 40 years on, with its horse-drawn manual pump and the accompanying hand-drawn truck which carried the hoses.

92.   The fire brigade in 1920, still with a horse-drawn engine but with a powerful steam pump attached. The two horses belonged to a local undertaker, so if a fire occurred whilst the horses were at a funeral, two others were borrowed from Bourners, the local carriers and coal merchants.

93. A very much later photograph of the Uckfield Auxiliary Fire Service, taken during the 1939-45 War. The date explains the masking of the name over the fire station.

94.   Market day. Note the policeman keeping a friendly eye on things, and the two men taking a rest on the high kerb.

95.   Mr. J. F. Bishop, another long-established butcher of Uckfield, holding two prize bullocks at Uckfield market in 1929, two years before it closed down.

96. The water tower, built in 1903 near to the site of Uckfield House, now demolished and the site of Manor Park Housing Estate. The water works at that time were at Hempstead, where water from artesian wells was pumped to a reservoir near Uckfield House. In 1903 an extra well and pumping house were added at the works, and the water tower at the reservoir. Many Uckfield people remember the sweet taste of the water when this was its source.

97. The Uckfield Hospital. Known originally as the Cottage Hospital, it was built for the town by R. J. Streatfeild in 1881. It was run by a Management Committee and a lady superintendent, and was supported partly by patients' fees and partly by voluntary subscriptions. The 15th Annual Report issued in August 1896 states that 37 cases were admitted during the year, and finishes with the following news: 'In consequence of slightly increased expenses during the past year, it is found necessary to draw £25 from the Reserve Fund in the P.O. Savings Bank, which amounts to nearly £152.' How things have changed in 100 years!

98. The clinic babies, *c*.1930. The happy mums and bonny babies of Uckfield, photographed in what were the Grammar School playing fields, now the site of the library and town car park.

Churches

99.   A drawing of the old church at Uckfield, before it was taken down in 1839 and a new church built the following year. The earliest reference to a chapel in Uckfield was in 1291 in the valuation of Pope Nicholas. Until 1846 it was a chapel-of-ease to Buxted and was served by the same incumbent. In 1846 Uckfield became a separate parish with its own perpetual curate who was declared Rector in 1865, the appointment being in the gift of the Archbishop of Canterbury. Further alterations to the church were carried out in 1889.

100.   The south side of Uckfield church in 1869. This shows the church before the addition of the lower entrance in the churchyard wall, before the building of the Sanctuary extension, with no south-west door to the church, and with only one clock face on the steeple (four faces were installed in 1894). It also shows, we believe, a very young and small yew tree, the tree which grew into a large and magnificent landmark admired by visitors and residents alike but which was totally destroyed by the hurricane of October 1987.

Uckfield Parish Church Bells before being recast 1905

101. Uckfield parish church bells, a peal of eight, being loaded at the railway station in 1905, on their way to be re-cast by Messrs. Mears and Stainbank at their Whitechapel Foundry. Mr. Wilkinson, the station porter, is in the background.

102. The Roman Catholic church was originally situated at Ringles Cross, under the patronage of the Duchess of Norfolk, who was also patroness of Herons Ghyll Roman Catholic church. In the early 1880s a temporary iron church and attached school was built on three-quarters of an acre of ground in Church Street, Uckfield. In 1896 more permanent and substantial buildings were erected on the site, which can just be seen on this 1945 photograph. In 1946 St Michael's College, New Town, was purchased and a new church built in 1957.

103. The new Roman Catholic church, New Town. The foundation stone was laid on 31 May and the solemn consecration took place on 21 September 1961.

104. St Saviour's church, Framfield Road, *c.*1905. This small church was built on land given by the Hon. Henry B. Portman of Buxted Park 'for the accommodation of residents in this growing part of the Town' (*Brooker's Guide* 1904). The Bishop of Chichester performed the dedication service on 18 November 1904 and it remained in use until 1971.

105. Christ Church, Ridgewood. This small church was built in 1876 on a site given by Mr. R. J. Streatfeild, and he and the Rev. E. T. Cardale shared the expense of building the church. It remained in use until 1969. Ridgewood School, long-closed and now a farm cottage, is shown on the opposite bank.

106. An architect's impression of the Congregational church – now the United Reformed church – which was built in its present position on the corner of Framfield Road, New Town, in 1866 at a cost of £2,300.

Schools

107.   Mountfield Preparatory School, New Town. These happy little faces tell their own story! The two substantial semi-detached villas are to become eight one-bedroomed flats after extensive alterations in 1988.

108.   National School, Belmont Road, now known as Holy Cross Church of England School. The foundation stone was laid by the Squire on St George's Day 1850 and the school remained in use until about 1970, after a new building was erected further down Belmont Road in 1966. This was too small, even before it opened due to the population explosion in the area! This picture shows Miss Kitty Pierpoint's class in 1912. Miss Pierpoint joined the town's manual telephone exchange in 1923 to become the third telephonist.

109.   Uckfield Grammar School, Church Street, was founded by Dr. Anthony Saunders, whose will provided for the gratuitous education of 12 boys and the use of his library of 600 volumes. In 1755 the school was established under the title of Buxted and Uckfield Saunders Foundation by a scheme of the Court of Chancery whereby sons of tradesmen and respectable mechanics were admitted. The school also took private pupils but the 'foundationers' paid 2d. only per week for the use of slates and books.

110.   The unveiling of a memorial to the Old Boys of Uckfield Grammar School who died in the 1914-18 War. The plaque was later transferred to the north wall of the parish church when the school closed in 1930.

Recreation

111.   Uckfield Bonfire Society was formed in 1827 and continues today. The tar barrel in the front of the picture of the 1892 celebrations was lit and rolled down the High Street to the river. Mrs. L. Blackford, one of the Society's Presidents, is also one of Uckfield's longest standing traders. It is over half a century since she and her late husband started business in Eastbourne Road as coal and coke merchants and general carriers.

112. Carnival, 1911. An entry of farm yokels from Hadlow Down photographed by Mr. Windsor-Spice outside his shop (now Carouselle).

113. The first Carnival Queen in 1937 was Miss Peggy Rice from the harness maker's shop in the High Street. The title was then won by the girl selling the most tickets for the carnival. A float carried the queen and her attendants in the carnival procession. This photograph shows Stella Ashman with Pam Brooks (left) and Pat Virgo (right) after the war, when a panel of judges made the selection at a local dance.

114. Miss Measures of Cambridge Lodge had the Picture House built in 1916 but the presiding magistrate refused her a licence as he owned the cinema in Harcourt Road and feared opposition! The building was used as a garrison theatre until after 1920 when the licence was eventually granted. The Picture House now claims to be the oldest working cinema in Sussex.

115. Uckfield Laundry outing, 4 September 1922. A happy day out in the Kent-registered Leyland. The laundry in Framfield Road was one of the town's largest employers and continued until the 1960s, when new home laundry appliances led to its closure.

116. National Carol League, 1915/1920. The Uckfield branch collection of £487 17s. 6d. for St Dunstan's, organised by the parish church choirmaster, H. R. Revely, was the second largest in all England.

117. The Amateur Dramatic Club's performance of 'Yeomen of the Guard', 1914. This production in the Public Hall was the last before the war and a large proportion of the town was involved. Many lads taking part were on the Western Front in the Royal Sussex Regiment within the year.

118. One of the cast was George Stuart St John Smith, the well-known auctioneer, surveyor and estate agent, who had premises in the High Street.

119. Horticultural Show in the Drill Hall, 1920. The Horticultural Society is still flourishing. Since the Drill Hall was demolished, the show is now held in the Town Hall (formerly the Public Hall).

120. Father Fletcher's Band. In Brooker's Uckfield *Guide* of 1888 this is referred to as the original town band. It was formed by Rev. P. Fletcher, who was Priest-in-Charge of the Roman Catholic church in Uckfield, and he can be seen at the back, with the bandmaster, Mr. James Haestier, on his right.

121. The town still has a band, now known as the Uckfield Industries Band.

122. Girl Guide Rally at Luxford's Field, July 1921. Guiding has always been popular in Uckfield and there are several companies in the town today. The founder, the late Lady Olave Baden-Powell, was baptised at St Margaret's, Buxted, where she addressed a Guide Rally in 1970. The house in the centre of this picture, 'The Wakelyns', was demolished between the wars.

123. Uckfield Wolf Cubs. Miss Streatfeild (the Squire's daughter) is seen here with the pack in 1922. Older gentlemen of the parish still remember her with respect and affection.

124. This photograph shows a popular run of the Uckfield Cycling Club on All Fools' Day 1932. The Club closed about 25 years ago, when the private motor car began to dominate the roads, but despite the hills in the town there are still plenty of cycles to be seen.

125. Uckfield football team won the Sussex Junior Cup and Humblecroft's Cup in the 1906/7 season.

126. The Bowls Club greens were at the rear of Charles Bellingham's Holly Bush Coffee Tavern in the High Street (demolished and now under the Bell Walk shopping precincts). Bowls was a popular pastime in the early years of this century.

127.   Meet at Uckfield, outside the *Bridge Hotel* (now the *Prince Regent*) – another excellent photograph by Mr. J. Frisby.

128.   The Uckfield Chamber of Commerce Ball, *c*.1932, held in the Public Hall in the days when a small country town still dressed up for its local functions and turned out in great numbers to enjoy themselves. Seated on the floor are the organising committee: (left to right) Rex Nicks, Jeff Clarke, Frank Fuller, Vic Jarvis and Bert Colbourne. Seated in the middle behind them are Mr. Ditch, a local dentist, and his wife.

129. The Walking Match, *c.*1920. This was an annual event and the competitors walked from Uckfield to Cross-in-Hand and back.

Special Events

130.   The Coronation of King George V and Queen Mary in 1911. Festivities were held in the Victoria Pleasure Ground to celebrate the event. These included bobbing for treacle rolls and a large bonfire in the evening.

131.   Opening of the Victoria Pleasure Ground, 21 April 1897. The recreational ground was given by the Squire, R. J. Streatfeild, to mark Queen Victoria's Diamond Jubilee. Note the large banner of the Tunbridge Wells Equitable Society, to which many townsfolk belonged.

132.   Scout's funeral, 12 March 1911. Scout Hazelden, who lived in Framfield Road, was a paper boy for W. H. Smith and Son of the station bookstall. He ran from the south platform across the railway line to pick up some papers from the north platform and was struck and killed by an oncoming train.

133.   Five local cadets. The cadets met in St Saviour's Hall, Framfield Road, until about 1920. George Thorpe worked for his father at 53 Framfield Road (now Mrs. M. M. Britton's hairdressing salon) which was then a butcher's shop, until he emigrated to Australia. The other lads stayed in Uckfield.

134.   The Air Raid Wardens, Fire Watchers and Civil Defence team, *c.*1940.

135. & 136. Floods in Mill Lane (*above*) and lower High Street (*below*), 1943. Uckfield has been seriously flooded seven times this century: 16 January 1918, 16 November 1929, 25 January 1939, 14 January 1943, 28 November 1952, 3 November 1960 and 22 November 1974. In 1974 Keymarket Supermarket had stock washed out of the shop and children gathered bananas on the flood waters! Southern Water Authority have since carried out remedial work to prevent flooding on this scale again.

137. Princess Victoria, Empress of Germany, planting a tree in Maresfield Recreation Ground in 1897 to commemorate her mother's Diamond Jubilee.

138. Queen Mary pictured with her friend, the Hon. Mrs. Nellie Ionides, escorted by the Rev. K. MacDermott, on one of her private visits to Buxted Park. She and Mrs. Ionides shared a love of collecting antiques.

139. Uckfield House, the home of Lord and Lady Nevill, was at the northern end of the town. The Queen and members of the royal family were frequent visitors. It was following a weekend here that the announcement that Princess Margaret would not marry Group Captain Peter Townsend was issued. Lord Rupert was secretary to Prince Philip and represented Uckfield on the East Sussex County Council. In 1964 planning permission was surprisingly granted for a large new housing estate on the site to be known as Manor Park.

140. H.M. The Queen leaving Uckfield parish church with the Rev. C. W. F. Bennett on one of her private visits to Lord and Lady Nevill. The royal train came to Uckfield to take the Queen to Aberfan to the scene of the coal tip disaster in the 1960s.

141. & 142. Horsted church and toll cottage. Lord and Lady Rupert Nevill took up residence at Horsted Place in 1964, following the deaths of Mr. and Mrs. Francis Barchard, for whom George Myers built this gothic mansion. Mature trees and shrubs were brought from Uckfield House and replanted, including a myrtle tree grown from a sprig from Queen Victoria's wedding bouquet.

New Estates and Constructions

143.   Keld Close, 1937. This photograph was taken from the hose tower at Uckfield fire station. Building work was done by the local firm, Durrant Bros. Keld Avenue followed shortly afterwards and Keld Drive was built in 1963 on the site of Mr. Taylor's chicken farm.

144.   These two young ladies were photographed in the early years of this century at the bottom of Pudding Cake Lane. A large council housing estate, Church Coombe estate, was built here by Uckfield Rural District Council just after the last war.

UCKFIELD,
FIELD WALK & CHURCH.

145. Manor Park estate. The derelict gamekeeper's cottage on the edge of Buxted Park made way for more new houses by Federated Homes Ltd.

146. The open ground in this picture is part of a new estate developed in 1985/6 and known as The Rydings. New road names recall the past; for example, Farriers Way, Forge Rise, and Bridge Farm Road.

147. Maresfield Mill Pond. A roundabout was constructed in 1985 at Budletts as part of the Uckfield by-pass scheme to join the A22, A26 and A272. This was the site of one of the finest flour mills in the district, which was burnt down in 1878 whilst in the ownership of Mr. John Hill.

148. This photograph, taken from 'Rest Harrow' (the middle portion of Prince Munster's stable block, now known as the Coach House), shows the unspoilt meadow of Maresfield Park. The land was then owned by Edward Wadsworth, R. A., who lived in the Dairy House and painted the panels in the *Queen Mary* liner. Bernard Howe (of Fletching) introduced one of the early combine harvesters in this field and residents gathered to see the wonderful new machine! Henry Boots' Georgian-style luxury houses were built here in 1963.

The Villages

149.   The main street of Fletching is little
changed from this photograph taken nearly
a century ago in 1890. It is one of the most
picturesque and well kept villages in Sussex.
Simon de Montfort is said to have camped
here with his army and prayed in the church
on the eve of the Battle of Lewes in 1264.

150.   The *New Inn*, Hadlow Down, was built
in 1887 and Mr. Markwick was landlord
until 1912. He kept beagles in the rear fields,
and iron nails where he hung meat on the
oak trees can still be seen. The present
proprietors are brother and sister Gerald
Standen and Dawn Johnson, who took over
the licence from their father George and
grandfather Thomas. Time has indeed stood
still at this public house, where real ale is
served.

151.   The *White Hart*, Buxted. Buxted is a two-part village. The earlier settlement was around the church of St Margaret the Queen in Buxted Park, near where Ralph Hogge cast the first cannon. Buxted Park Mansion is reached through an avenue of lime trees in a deer park. The other part of Buxted developed after 1858, when the railway came.

152.   Buxted High Street: the later development near the station. Miller's Hygienic Bakery operated here from about 1900 until 1938. The business was started by Lewis Miller and taken over in 1919 by his son-in-law, Douglas Edwards.

153. Christ Church, Fairwarp. The church stands on high, open ground in the heart of Ashdown Forest – the clock and bells can be heard for miles around. This photograph was taken in 1930 before the church tower was added in 1937. In 1940 the church suffered damage by enemy action.

154. Nutley is another forest village. Its wooden windmill (the open trestle post type) ceased commercial use in 1908, but has been restored by Uckfield and District Preservation Society. The society was awarded a European Architectural Heritage Year Award for this work in 1975.

155. The church of St Thomas à Becket, Framfield, about 1900. The church was built in the early 13th century and is still the focal point of the village, approached by a row of neat Tudor cottages.

156. & 157.   In 1912 archaeologists from all over the world gathered in Uckfield public hall for Charles Dawson, a local solicitor, to display his 'find', a skull of Dawn Man, found at Barkham Manor, Piltdown. It was a gala day for Uckfield and Mr. and Mrs. F. J. Bellingham of the High Street Central Tearooms catered for the dignitaries. Half a century later, the Piltdown Man was proved a fake. The pictures show (above) Charles Dawson with Mr. Frisby on site to photograph the archaeologists at work (below).

158.   Battalion Parade, Maresfield Camp Park, 1917. In 1941 Maresfield again became a military village. This time, the camp site was Batts Road, where it remained until its closure in the 1970s. During the last war, King George VI inspected the troops prior to D-Day on Maresfield recreation ground.

159.   Main Drive, Maresfield Park. This fine avenue of lime trees led to the Manor House and its service buildings. Sadly, the hurricane of 16 October 1987 uprooted most of the trees.

160. Count and Countess Alexander Munster lived in Maresfield Park for about 30 years until the outbreak of war in 1914, when they returned to Germany.

161. Stable hands round the well at Maresfield Park. Prince Munster's crest can be seen on the stable block behind. The army requisitioned the building during the Great War and W.A.A.C.s were billeted here. One service lady married Alfred Brown of Tanyard Farm, Underhill, Maresfield, and became a well-known personality in the village. She pushed a churn in a pram and ladled milk from it into customers' jugs.

162. The steep hill on the north side of the *Chequers Inn* leads to a quiet and picturesque corner of the village known as Underhill. In earlier days, this was one of the industrial areas, where the forge and wheelwrights were to be found.

163.   Isfield Forge operated into the 1960s and was demolished about 1970, when the Forge House was converted.

164.   Isfield Mill in the 1920s. The family business of Dickson & Church acquired the mill in 1937 and continues to trade today.

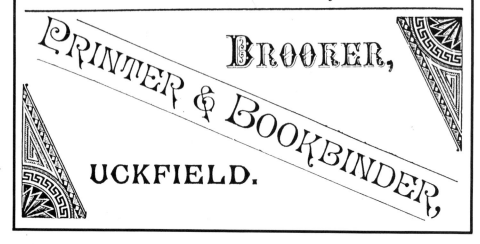